Ellen Turlington Johnston

Library of Congress Catalog Card Number: 74-14960

ISBN 0-87716-057-0

For my high school principal who retired this past spring, Mr. W. A. Hough, a beautiful, sensitive, loving human being, whose warm understanding and gentle acceptance of sometimes-unorthodox, often-discombobulated me made it possible for me to teach, to learn, to love, and—hopefully—to grow;

For Barbara, Reed, and Pat;

For Aggie, Adelyn, Cindy, and all who believed this book *would* be:

And for my mother, who showed me—a very long time ago—how to look, to *see*; to listen, to *hear;* to experience, to *feel;* and how to write it down.

PREFACE

This book is a nonfiction narrative that happens to be written in verse.

It is a story of frustration, futility, failure, and disillusionment. It is a story, also, of faith, friendship, forgiveness, and warm moments. And it is a story of hope – always hope.

The protagonist? It is Youth. It is Jimmy and Mike and Angela, groping for purpose and meaning, struggling for identity, for recognition, for belonging in the microcosm of the classroom. It is the Adult, Mrs. J. or Mr. B. or Miss S., groping for purpose and meaning, struggling to teach, to understand, to *reach* our brave young seekers.

So What Happened To You? presents many questions. You outside the classroom doors ask, "Why?" We – inside – ask, "Why?" This book offers no answers. It offers only the truth. Each "chapter" records an incident – the hole-punchers, the Christmas mop, the riot, the missing five-dollar bill – as it happened; or an impression as I experienced it. After you have read the book, some of the *why's* you may be closer to answering than *before* you lived through these things with me.

I dedicate this book to my fellow-teachers everywhere, for whom many of the "chapters" will strike well-known, if sometimes cacaphonous, chords; and to our students, who have taught us what "everything's *really* about."

I wrote this book because I *had* to.

> ". . . . I had to tell it; had to try
> To write it, cage experience in form
> So someone else could share these things with us,
> Could *feel* them, live them with us, and could know
> The very special way it is . . . " That's why.

With love,

Mrs. J

CONTENTS

SO WHAT HAPPENED TO *YOU?*

DON'T BLOW YOUR "MEAN"

Before I went into the Blackboard Jungle, I asked some school teachers what was the secret to teaching good,
Like a school teacher should.
(I was scared, unsure, and terribly green.)
And every teacher I asked told me emphatically,
"BE MEAN." And they didn't *mean* be mean erratically.
I asked, "What do you mean, "mean"?
They answered, "Whatever you do, DON'T SMILE.
At least, not for a very, very long while.
Perhaps, you could smile *once*, as you bid them goodbye for Christmas, at the very earliest;
Until then, be your unsmilingest-surliest."

I thought about it and thought about it, and figured I could do it.
But it happened that on the first day in the first five minutes . . .
I BLEW IT!
I stood there on my side of the desk and watched those thirty-five kids sitting in their places;
And as I looked over that seething sea of scared, cocky, sad-happy, pimply, fuzzy, questioning faces,
There was NO way
I could NOT smile.
Christmas? I couldn't wait 'till *Hallowe'en*!
I must hold the world's record for the shortest time a schoolteacher ever maintained her "mean."
To be perfectly honest, I didn't wait *five* minutes; it was more like two,
And that tipped them right off that I wasn't doing the way they knew good and well a school teacher's *supposed* to do.
They figured right then I was going to be a pushover, and that is a shame,
Because I really have got all the makings of a tough-teacher-type-no-nonsense kind-of-a-dame.
In fact, one tenth grader told me the first time he saw me, he – (the poor thing) – held his breath;
I looked so tall and tough and *mean*, he was scared half to death.

That is, until I had to go and smile; then he decided I wasn't going to be mean – he just knew it.
So you see, I *did* have the fight won, but I threw it!

That first year, I had a few minor problems like spitballs, and catcalls, and a couple of young men left through the window one day when they *didn't* even have an *excuse*!
And the kids passed notes in class, and heavens knows *what* all; you might say, I suffered a good bit of abuse.
But things are ever so much better, now I've learned the name of the game, 'though there is still a bit of insubordination from a few of my livelier students;
And I imagine there are some who consider that I handle my classes with rather a too light-hearted imprudence.
But the funny thing is that – not any more now – do I ever *feel* out of control;
It has to do with what you're aiming for – and how – and it's because my top-priority goal
Is to show kids that school doesn't have to be boredom and slavery, with me a dictator above them,
And that I'm someone who wants them to think and to feel and enjoy; I want to talk with, listen to, most of all – love them.
At first it was hard, because I thought it important that they love me, too.
But now, it doesn't really bother that probably a good many more of them *don't* than *do*.

See, I've found out a whole lot of kids will run rough-shod over you if you don't police them;
Then, they write in your Annual: "You should have been meaner," because you didn't yell and stamp your foot and frown alot, and occasionally fleece them.
But if I can – every now and again – show one cutting-up, nervy, bad-mouthing, anti-teacher, *un*lovable kid
That *I* loved him – (though God knows, he didn't *deserve* it) – then it makes up for all the smiling and loving that I ever did.

I LOVE YOU

You are sullen,
And alot of people can't stand you.
You are sneaky.
You cheat,
And lie alot.
You steal things,
And you don't look nice.
You smell bad, too.

I love you.

I smile at you.
But you don't believe it,
Or accept it,
Or want it.

> "How can that woman love me?
> My mother is a whore.
> My sister, too."

You don't know that I know.
But I do.
And I love you.

DO YOU REMEMBER ME, BERNICE GRENADINE?

Do you remember me, Miss Grenadine?
I remember you. Are you teaching still?
Still rated, as teachers go, "cracker-jack"?
They told me you were, way back
When you were assigned to supervise my student-teaching,
  Or practice teaching . . .
  (Call it what you will . . .)
Do you remember? I remember well.

You were sharp all right, Miss Bernice Grenadine.
You ran a real tight ship, too.
I mean . . . those kids toed the line for you.
Me . . . I toed the line, too.

I was no kid. But I was eager like a kid
Who, on Christmas morning, can't wait
To get to that shimmery tree.
I was like a colt, whinnying at the gate.
I was *that* eager to get in there and take over the class.
(My bumbling excitement seemed foolish to you, I guess.)

So one day, as I bridled at the bit,
You said, "All right. It's yours. Take it.
But remember, handle the disciple problems in the room – yourself.
Never, never send anyone out!"

Who me? Discipline problems? I put every doubt
Right up there on the shelf.
Hadn't my Education Professor promised there'd be none?
All you had to do was "Motivate."
Problems? Oh no. This would be fun.

I couldn't wait!

But things didn't go too well for me, Miss Grenadine.
I wonder . . . do you recall?
They went from not-too-bad, at first,
  To impossible,
  Worse than worst.

Especially Jimmy, who fit no mold at all;
He was like a panther in a cage that's too small.
I scolded Jimmy every day. Do it myself? Honest, I tried.
But on Wednesday of my third week, I finally sighed,
    "Jimmy, go to the office and get a paddling."
Jimmy went to the office.
Me – I went to the ladies' room . . . and cried.

Later, I saw a girl from that class – Betty Sue.
I told her how terrible I felt for sending Jimmy out,
    (Which you – remember? – told me *never* to do,
    So I knew it was all wrong);
Betty Sue said: "But Miss Grenadine's sent him ten-eleven times
    already this year –
    Before you were here.
    We 'been wondering what took you so long!"

Do you remember *me* Bernice Grenadine?
I'll ALWAYS remember YOU.

WONDERFULNESS

Bulletin boards are a must, you may know;
You've got to have something right up there to *show*,
So if a proud parent, or some school official
Should drop by to visit, they'll give a soft whistle
And say to you later, "I simply *adored*
Your int'resting, colorful bulletin board!"

The very first year that ever I taught
I knew that if I was to be worth my salt,
I'd have a perpetual, wondrous sight
All painted and pasted up there to look bright;
And make it look like we did really great stuff
All day in the classroom. As kids say, look "tough."

I forged right ahead with a, "Come on! Let's go!
It's time for the bulletin board thing, you know!"
I heard some low groans and some dirty words, too;
My bulletin board kick was *not* getting through.
Then somebody snickered . . . . out loud – so I'd hear,
"It was just one big bulletin board all *last* year!"

Well, it wasn't just then that I dared do my thing;
I was simply too new to try out my own wings.
But before very long I was all up to *here*
With bulletin boards, and I got this idea.

We had a traditional board on the wall
With pictures of authors we'd studied, and all.
It was time for a change, so I grabbed up a rose
That somebody'd brought me, and up on my toes
I ripped off the old, and with no reservation
I stapled that rose to the board – a sensation!
Then I picked up a part of a pencil – all split –
Right up on the board with scotch tape, and it fit!

A broken broom handle tied up the next place,
A messed-up eraser, that wouldn't erase.
By now, all the students had got in the swing,
And *all* of us bulletin-boarded our thing.

Part of a love note – snatched – torn up by me
Went next to the dead rose, significantly.
A dirty blue beanie left under a chair –
We stapled *it* up, and it looked good up there.

A cheat sheet (used) next, typed up nice and neat
That somebody went off and left in his seat;
A small vial of perfume, "Pink Passion" the name;
A broken-up comb, and a small checkers game.

Two cards someone lost – a black Jack, a red King
Were next. They went well with the scheme of the thing.
A Superman funny book, big wad of gum;
Then we taped up a rather large Oreo crumb.

It said something REAL, and there wasn't a doubt
Our collage was what everything's *really* about.
You may well suppose that the thing was a mess,
But *we* loved it and called our board: "WONDERFULNESS."

HERO

A golden bronze zig-zag . . . zig-zag
Of lightning – YOU.
A FLASH – down
across down . . . over. SCORE!

Screaming stands adore their hero – YOU.
YOU - worshipped.
YOU - loved.
(Never mind that adoration looms
In direct proportion to
The yardage gained by you
Each Friday night . . .
That's all right.)
YOU are loved . . . never mind *why*.
YOU are the glitter in a coed's eye,
(If she aims *really* high.)

We wrote some odes to you one day, for fun:
"Hail to thee, O Shelton Howard,
Epic hero; ne'er a coward.
Winged sandals gird they feet.
Hail, O Hail . . ." and on like that.

(Now the words ring hollow . . . flat.)

God, I wish we'd praised not what you'd *done* –
HERO Shelton, mighty football star –
But praised the quiet *human being* you are,
The *inside* you, the really you,
(But that's the you we hardly knew at all;
And so . . . we praised your prowess with the ball.)

Then ONWARD, UP to college, where there'd be
More glory, praise, and more idolotry.
HERO – not so tall, so big, but *fast*!

It didn't last.

You came back Christmas-time, came to my class.
"How's the football hero now?" I asked.

You kind of ducked your head.
"I haven't played," you said.
"The physical - they found a murmur then.
And so . . . I haven't played again.
And now," (you said it in a factual way),
"No one looks up to me;
Not anymore, Miz. J."

"Oh, Shelton, that's not true!
I always . . . we all, *all* look up to you!"

But as you turned, so quietly, to leave,
Your star – all tarnished – that was when I knew
You never could – or ever would – believe
That what I said was true.

MISERY

My friend, do you know what real misery is,
When all the world's a bummer, all's amiss?
I'll tell you, friend, *real* misery is *this*:

It's when you wear your panty-hose to school,
(For this is something that I always do),
But *this* day – what an uncontested fool,
Oh, what a rotten, ill-begotten trip! –
You fail to wear your us'al NON-cling slip.
And on that day – (it HURTS to reminisce) –
You wear a dress that is a tight-ish fit.
Ah, what a sheer, unmitigated mess!
(You see, it would have been all right – that dress –
Without a CLINGING slip worn under it.)

Then, all day long it's misery . . . despair . . .
For all day long you have to stand up there
In front of eyes-don't-*won't*-deceive them classes;
And you are devastatingly aware
That nobody out there – not *one* – needs glasses
To see that Teacher wears a CLINGING slip,
A twisting, riding, crawling thing that climbs,
And wriggles, writhes, then clusters 'round her hip.
And then – before they figure *that* – post haste,
It's only just a tiny little time
Until it hunches, bunches 'round your waist.

Now, all your students know you're under stress;
You know that they can see *right through* your dress,
And see that inner-tubish looking mess
All scrunched around your middle under it.

And so, all drenched in deepest misery,
Grotesque, misshapen, hopeless; helplessly
You crawl, whipped-down, behind your desk and sit.

You will not move from there, your last refuge;
You can not, will not, dare not, do not budge.
You give them "busy" work, and then you pray
That somehow, *sometime*, God will end this day.

THE CHRISTMAS MOP

This is a Christmas story, (and it's true),
About a mop,
You know, with long strings at the top –
Or bottom –
Depending on your point of view.
It was in a corner in a school room.
Someone left it there after "Clean-Up Week."
That – and a broom.
But they took the broom off somewhere.
That left the mop.
And nobody wanted it . . .
Or needed it . . .
Or loved it.
  (To tell the truth
  It was ugly.)

****

It started getting Christmas time,
But I didn't *feel* Christmasy.
I just felt busy . . .
And harassed . . .
And *un*-spirited.
And there I was in that school room –
Me, and the desks and chairs,
And lots of kids, coming and going,
And the little mop . . . in the corner,
Alone . . . unwanted . . . ugly.

So I stood it up
With the strings hanging down;
Some silvery icicles
I laced all through it.
Tiny, shiny balls –
Red and green –
I hung on to it.

Tinsel for the pole,
Around and around.
A star on top
For a crown.

Now, my little mop had a soul . . .
A sparkle . . .
A sheen.
It said BELONGING;
And it said CARING:
And it said LOVE;
And it said . . . . .CHRISTMAS.

I had to tell you.
I don't know just why.
I suppose . . .
It's because I found out
You can look and look for Christmas,
And there it is all along
Right under your nose
In a corner,
Hoping you'll see . . . and stop.
Just like my
  Ugly
  Little
  Lonely
  Mop.

MY SPECIAL FRIEND

I had a special friend in study hall –
a small, brown girl; a quiet kid.
 I liked her.
 She liked me.
She helped me, too. She took the roll,
and, sometimes, tidied up my desk a bit,
(if it needed it),
which – alot of times – it did.
 I was interested in her.
 She was interested in me.
She liked to look at the pictures of my three
that were in my wallet.
If someone new came in the room,
she'd ask to see my wallet,
so she could show them the pictures of my children.
 Which pleased her.
 And pleased me.
One day, my friend was looking at the pictures again,
and she opened up the change part of my wallet.
There were: a ten, a five, two ones,
three quarters, a dime, two pennies.
 She said, "Oh!"
 I said to her, "That's grocery money. . . ."
She closed up the change part then,
and gave my wallet back again.

A little later, two of her friends came in,
and she said, "Let me show them your children."
So she took the wallet.
I didn't watch her – (she stood behind me) –
because she was my friend,
and she had to know I trusted her.
 That was important to her.
 And important to me.
In a little while, then,
she gave my wallet back again.

And I was afraid.

When she wasn't looking at me,
I looked inside the change part – quick.
There were: a ten, ... two ones,
three quarters, a dime, two pennies.
No more.
I felt sick.

With wide gestures, I looked all over the desk,
all around on the floor.
But I knew.
And *she* knew.
She knew that *I* knew, too.

I said – quietly,
"Angela, by any chance did you see my five dollar bill?"
She didn't really say.
She kind of shook her head and looked away.
I looked for it some more,
all over the desk,
all around the floor.

Then I looked at her for a long time.
I said – softly,
"Angela, did you *take* my five dollar bill?"
She made a kind of noise that sounded like, "No."
But she never looked at me.

I knew.
And *she* knew.
She knew that *I* knew, too.

We both knew why it would be a long, long time
before she could be my special friend
again.

IF YOU CAN'T MOTIVATE THE LITTLE DARLINGS *ONE* WAY, MOTIVATE THEM *ANOTHER*

AUTHOR'S NOTE: This was written, during my second year of teaching, in tribute and thanks to a junior-high principal, who recognized my problems with a forty pupil, Special Education (70 and below I.Q.) eighth-period study hall, and compassionately relieved me of half the class.

I had figured there was no way out, so I had not complained. It was just – I cried alot.

Too, it should be noted here that Dr. Hansil and I had a running joke on this magic word, "motivation," that you learn all about in your required Education courses, but that's a whole lot easier *said* than *done*!

'Never wanted to cry "Uncle,"
'Never meant to wave a flag.
Still, you came to my assistance
With my "cultural-ish lag."

Yes, that "study" hall *was* . . . different,
'Almost lost my sense of humorous.
The Special Ed's *were* special,
And especially too *numerous*!

I told adventure stories,
Read of happy-ever-afters.
And while I entertained, the *kids*
Were swinging from the rafters.

I shouted and I paddled.
Though I couldn't *ever* hate them,
They left me awf'ly addled
'Cause I couldn't MOTIVATE them!?!?

So thank *you* for "motivating" half of the little darlings home every afternoon *before* eighth period.

Nicest Christmas present I ever had!

Mrs. J.

PREFACE – TO OUR YOUNG BUILDERS

It was the year of the riots in the Charlotte-Mecklenburg school system, where busing had been fully implemented the year before. Our riot hadn't struck yet, (it did about three weeks after I had written this poem), but tension was high and trouble was erupting in schools all around us.

As we talked one day in my Creative Writing class about Blacks and Whites getting along and *not* getting along; as the students aired their gripes and hurts, jealousies and resentments, it suddenly occurred to me that nobody had given these young people credit for the giant steps they *had* made. They had been doing something that never had been done before here: learning, living, playing, working for five days a week with people of another race, people they had never known or understood, (or even *been* with), until—suddenly, traumatically—it was thrust upon them.

I told these young people that I thought it was really SOMEthing – how far they had come. You should have seen their faces!

And then I knew I had to go home and write about it.

So I did. This is it.

And what, you may wonder, was my reaction to the riot that happened *after* I wrote my tribute? I was discouraged. It was a falling-back, a stumbling. But the building, I knew, would go on. And, so it has.

TO OUR YOUNG BUILDERS

You are the heroes – You –
You young. You black. You white. You beautiful.
But you don't know it, do you?
Maybe it's because we have not told you
That you are taking giant steps each day;
You are pioneers who blaze the way
For others coming on.

You are the ones who build the bridges now
Across the canyons of
Man's inhumanity to man.
Block by block and beam by beam, your work
Is tortuous and treacherous and slow.

You grow impatient, too.
But only stop. Look back and see
How far you've come in just so little years.
Across the plains of hate, you're building love.
And there is anguish, anger, yes, and fear;
But build you must – and can.
And over peaks of ignorance you scale,
Pulling after some who slip and lose
A toe-hold here, a hand-hold there.
You pull the faltering. You pull the ones
Who fear a change, because they are not sure
Of *who* they are . . . or *what* they are . . . or *where*.

We never told you, and you do not know
That you are giants building giant bridges
Between two worlds.
You see, *our* world was "safe." We had it made."
We older ones had pigeon holes for this,
And cubby holes for that. We knew our "place,"
And everybody else's too, we thought.
And we were soft, complacent in *our* world,
Our little safe and tidy scheme of things.

But you – you black, you white, you young, you brave –
Are breaking down the barriers and seeing
Through eyes – ('though sometimes angered, clouded some
By things you've learned before, by talk at home
From those who do not know) – eyes that see
Not black, not white, but just a human being.

Scaling mountains is not ever easy;
Building giant bridges makes you hurt.
The blisters of frustration grow and fester.
Yes . . . tears there are . . . and anger. Yes . . . despair
When you fall back or stumble in the dirt
Of bigotry from those who do not dare
To be like you.

But still you build. Your bridge grows straight and true.
And you, the engineers, the architects;
And you, the young surveyors and the crew,
Are making it across because you're strong.
And when the bigoted shout, "NO! You can't!"
Your bridge between two worlds shouts, back, "You're wrong!"

SAY?

DID YOU EVER SEE A RIOT?

Say?

Where kids you know and love and teach everyday

runandrunandrunandrunandrun

and

SCREEEEEEEEEEEEAM

and

SLAMSLAMSLAMSLAMSLAMSLAMSLAMSLAM
BANGSMASHBANGSMASHBANGSMASH
doors

andyankandpullandtearandwrenchbookspapersgymshoesshorts
booksnotebookspapersbookspapersbookspapersbookspapers

out of lockers

and

RIPRIPRIPRIPRIPRIPTEARANDRIPTEARANDRIP
posterspicturespapers
maps
murals
calendars
schedules
posterspaperspicturesmuralsmapsposterspictures

off walls

and

S T A M P E D E

in the halls halls halls halls halls

and

SMAAAAAAAAAAAAAAAASH
windows

and

SCREAMandSCREAMandSCREAMandSCREAM

and

beatbeatbeatbeatbeat – up a girl
who gets
in
the
WAY
in the WAY

IN THE WAY –

(and all she was doing was coming out of the bathroom.)

Say?

HAVE YOU EVER SEEN A RIOT?

And run alongside the tall, good-looking young man you know who leads it – or *did* lead it . . . at first . . . *No* one *leads* it now – not *now*. And you know him and teach him – except he doesn't look like you ever *saw* him
look before . . . .

And you beg him to stop it . . . STOP THEM . . . You understand what he wants, but THIS isn't the . . .

And he SHOUTS – angry . . . exultant?
in a voice you never
heard before –

CAN'T

TOO LATE, MAN!

CAN'T STOP 'EM NOW.

NOBODY CAN

NO WAY!

Say?

DID *YOU* EVER SEE A RIOT?

And run beside a skinny-legged fifteen-year old
who's so scared to death
she's almost
white.

And she
stops
running . . .
and . . . she's
all
out
of
breath . . .
and she says to you in a little little voice –
It wasn't 'sposed to be this way . . .
I don't know how it began . . .

See – we were all just standing there . . . in the cafeteria . . . having this meeting . . . and . . . then . . .

somebody
started
running . . . .

and then so did . . . so did . . . so . . .
everybody just ranandranandranandranandran
they shouted SHOUTED and they . . . and we
shouted we SHOUTED WE SHOUTED SHOUTED . . .
RIGHT ON RIGHT ON RIGHTONRIGHTONRIGHTONRIGHTONRIGHTON
WE SHALL OVERCOME WE SHALL OVERCOMEWESHALL
OVER c o m e . . . .

we . . . .

I gotta go now –

all whispery, she

runs

away
with her skinny legs

and her scared eyes

and the little little voice . . .

It wasn't *'sposed* to be this way . . . .

DID YOU EVER *REALLY* **SEE** A RIOT?

Say?

EXTRA-CREDIT
(or IT'S TOO LATE, JOHN)

It comes *that* time again.
The nine-weeks tests are through.
Your grades are turned in – done.
It comes as no surprise
That here comes John, young John,
Who has not picked up paper,
Nor pencil, nor yet pen
Since grading time began.

He turns his big blue eyes,
(which you had not yet seen,
for they were closed in class
for nine weeks – every day),

Imploringly at you
And begs, "What can I do
For extra-credit? Say?
You see, I *gotta* pass.
How 'bout I do a theme
On Edgar Allan Poe?"

(Whom we have not mentioned in any way
The live-long year.
John does not know;
He did not hear.
But he does just *happen* to have this neat essay
On said Edgar Allan Poe,
Which his kid-sister did last year,
Which, he figures, *I* don't know.)

"It's too late, John.
My grades are done."

But John has *just* begun!

How 'bout I do a bulletin board?"

(But Jimmy beat him there.
He extra-credited it –
Yesterday –
With minutes – *just* to spare.)

"I'm sorry, John.
My grades are done."

"How 'bout I draw a picture. Look,
I'll draw a *bunch* – a whole scrap book!
and wash your board and empty your waste basket
and sweep your room and straighten your desk
and . . . ."

"It's too late, John.
My grades are done."

"How 'bout I *promise* to bring a pencil every day?
And listen and take down everything you say?
How 'bout from here on I *promise* to do good,
Then – this time – you could pass me. You know you could.
Or Dad'll take away my car and make me quit my job
and make me stay home nights and call me dumb and,
pro'bly, beat me up.
How 'bout – starting *tomorrow* – I do really good?"

"It's too late, John.
I'd pass you, if I could.
I really would.
But – tomorrow – a NEW day will dawn.
Then, you'll have *promises* to keep."

But . . . . tomorrow . . . .

John is fast asleep . . .
Again.
With *no* paper,
or pencil,
or pen.

I WAS RIGHT ABOUT YOU

You stuck your lower lip out at me
in class – the second day.
You were talking – loudly.
I asked you to move.
You snarled: "Make me."
"I will." I said. "Right away."

And I did.

The way you looked then,
with your lip out like that,
your jaw – like those old pictures
of Mussolini;
your head rared back,
all of you – rared back,
was too much. A caricature.
I looked at your brown eyes there . . .
too glaring
too defiant;
and I saw, beneath the glare,
something else.
I was softened.
It *was* there.
I was sure.

Oh, my dear young man,
you are a rotten actor, you know,
with your thin face,
your shoulder-length hair,
your lip sticking out – so.

Then, one day – in class – we talked . . .
all of us . . .
among ourselves;
about ourselves
about being loved,
and – especially – not being loved –

or even liked much.
For the first time, you talked to us . . .
With us.
You said: "My dad won't look at me in a crowd.
He's scared someone will know
I'm *his*."

We understood . . .
We, who you thought were strangers,
who you let share with you
the way it *is*
with you.

And we . . .
who you thought were strangers
loved your honesty . . .
understood your loneliness . . .
and even your lower lip,
which stuck out as you talked about
your dad and you.

And as you talked,
as we listened,
your lower lip did not stick out so much;
your head did not rare back so much.

******

Then . . . . today . . .
when I pulled out my desk drawer;
I mean pulled OUT – all the way –
and everything scattered,
everyone laughed.
It was pretty funny . . . . . . I guess.
Unexpected . . . so that they all laughed
at the scrambled mess . . .
and at me.
How did *you* know . . .

I was tired today,
a bit discouraged,
my sense of humor worn thin?
I *tried* to laugh – I did.

How did *you* know, then?

You came quietly,
gently picking up my drawer, replacing it.
Almost tenderly, you gathered up
my index cards . . .
staples . . .
thumbtacks . . .
broken chalk, paperclips, rubberbands . . .
my little, scratchy notes,
a calendar, a memo pad;
some library passes, erasers;
two ballpoint pens,
a lipstick I had . . .
and a pink comb with three teeth missing at one end.
You put them in my drawer for me
gently . . . almost tenderly.

You see,
I was right about you –
My dear, sensitive,
Loving,
Young friend.

EXPEDIENCY

The first time that I gave a test
I hoped the kids would do their best.
My trust . . . just ignorance – complete.
They did their *best* all right . . . to cheat!

I didn't monitor or pry;
I looked at floor, at wall, at sky.
'Much later learned – (someone told me) –
They actually passed the key!

The answer sheet upon my desk
Lay openly. I knew no risk.
But, enterprisingly, a lad
Had slipped it off. Then he had
Passed it quickly down each row,
Back and forth and to and fro.
Each young scholar, rapidly,
Used it expeditously.
Then it was slipped back, whilst I
Gazed at floor, at wall, at sky.

Cheating's IN, ah yes, my friend.
Any means to reach the end.
Use a system. *Any* way,
Make 100; make that "A."

Shocking? Yes. But, still, it's true.
Monkey see and monkey do.
For they learn it, I expect,
From the image *we* reflect.

MY LINE

One day I'm going to lead a line
That's long and straight and true and fine.
Just ME in front; behind – my class,
And NOBODY will stray or pass.

And NOBODY will bolt or run,
Not five or six, not even one.
There'll be no flaw; not one mistake,
No gap or hole or crack or break.

(You see, the lines I always lead
Are quite irregular, indeed,
With empty spaces here and there
Where someone got away somewhere.)

One day, I told this class of mine,
"A teacher *needs* to lead a line
That walks all nicely, straight and true – "
(It helps her *image* if they do.)

That day, assembly beckoned all.
Before we headed down the hall,
I emphasized my pressing need
About this line I hoped to lead.

A line to end *all* – my intent,
A perfect, ordered regiment.
The teachers would stand by to see
This wondrous line, led on by ME!

To lend the thing more dignity
I pledged I would not look to see
If any of my "soldiers" fled.
"I'll trust you, troops."
"Lead on!" they said.

We started out; I walked so *proud*;
They weren't unruly, crooked, loud.
Ah – discipline! Esprit de corps! . . .
As we filed past the rest room door.

I kept my word. My eyes were fast
As straight I marched my line right past
The smoking ramp, nor did I slack
Like Orpheus did – not *I* – look back!

And, finally, the march was done.
I turned, aglow, to thank each one
For his support. I counted, then.
Lost: twenty-some. Left? Nine or ten.

Afterward to MY LINE

I had read these poems to my homeroom class one day. It was three weeks later, "Teacher Appreciation Day" at North Mecklenburg High School. Each homeroom was to do something special, of their own invention, for their teacher. Many of the teachers received flowers. My class' gift to me was A Perfect Line.

At the beginning of the period, my students presented me with a paraphrased version of "My Line." (See next page.) Next, they pinned a badge on me. It read: "Perfect Line Leader/Awarded to E. Johnston, April 12, 1973." They said: "Lead us anywhere, Mrs. J.!"

So out the door we marched. There never has been so silent, so *in*-step, so straight-as-an-arrow, so PERFECT a line as MY LINE was that remarkable day. Up steps, down walk-ways, through halls, past rest rooms, past the smoking ramp we marched. As I looked back – ever so often, ever so *proud* – I saw, in the faces of my twenty-five students – such joy and pride and glowing beauty, born of doing something wonderful for somebody, that, as I wrote in my poem to them, (See next page), I won't be the same again.

P.S. Yes, there really *were* twenty-five students at the *end* of the march!

FROM MY HOMEROOM TO ME: THE LINE

" Our lady wanted to lead a line
That's long and straight and true and fine.
Our lady wanted to lead a line
That she could speak of from time to time.
Our lady wanted to lead a line
With her in front, and us behind;
With no empty spaces and no mistakes,
No cracks, no holes, no bumps, no brakes.
Just a line so proud and gay,
With Sally and Sue and Tommy and Jay.
So we, her class, decided to . . . .
Let her dream come very true,
A line that she could be proud of,
A line to remember,
A line that we all are proud to be a member.

To you, Mrs. Ellen Johnston, we present YOUR LINE. May this be the first of a long line of lines."

****

FROM ME TO MY HOMEROOM:

ONE PERFECT LINE

Today's the day I touched the stars and circled 'round the sun.
Like Haley's comet, I flew high, and trailing out behind –
My beautiful young followers, all beautifully in line,
  A perfect, glowing file of everything that's gently kind.

Today, I felt such love that I won't be the same again.

Today I soared, and my clay feet did not once touch the earth.
For, with the gift you gave to me, you made it all seem worth
  My thousand little trip-ups, my daily, foolish slip-ups,
  My earthly disappointments that happen now and then.

Today you were aligned with me, your young lives linked to mine.

From this day on, whenever I get caught in choppy seas,
And feel I may be drowning in the day's complexities,
I'll stop . . . and think of your young lives and what you brought
to mine . . .
And pull up to the stars again,
Holding tight to thoughts of when
You gave me my LOVE-LINE.

With a heart full of thanks to you for the most
beautiful line that ever was. I'll never, ever
forget what happened to me on April 12, 1973!

With love,
Mrs. J.

POOR BILL

Bill likes to play it very, very cool
At school.
He wants everyone to know
He is WITH it.
Real cool.
Tough.
Nobody can hurt *him*.
He won't take any stuff
Off anyone.

Oh, yes, Bill is WITH it.
He says:
Don't bug me, man.
and
Right on
and
Yeah, baby.

When he gets "down," Bill
Takes a pill.

Lots and lots of pills.
(His friend told me that one day he took twenty-three.)
And then he talks and talks and talks and talks,
And says nothing . . .
nothing . . .
nothing.

He gets too "up." So Bill
Takes a pill.
Lots and lots of pills.
And then he sleeps and sleeps and sleeps and sleeps,
And says nothing . . .
nothing . . .
nothing.

When Bill wants to be happy,
And forget
he's
Scared
and
Lonely,
He smokes a marijuana cigarette.

Bill wants to be WITH it.
Real cool.
Tough.

Poor Bill.
He never will.

ME – LOST AND FOUND

"ME.
Who am I?
What? Why?
Gotta find MYself – ME,"
They explain earnestly.

******

"I.
Who AM I?"
The *young* ME asked that, too.
Not – "Who are YOU?"
I, too, searched for ME,
Desperately,
My-SELF-ishly.

******

It's the sign
Of the times . . .

They sing:

Gotta be ME
Gotta be free.

Do MY thing!

Leave ME be.
I'll leave you be.

Gotta swing . . .
free,

Just ME.

Let ME move,
I'll find MY groove . . .

NOW!

But HOW?

S T R E T C H your M I N D, baby

Can't do?

How about a joint, or a little LSD, maybe,
to help you find
the real YOU.

NOW!

******

Me????

Yes, I found me . . .

Eventually.

HOW?

Finally . . .

I STOPPED searching
so desperately
for
ME,

With the capital "M,"
And the capital "E."

Then . . . .

I lost ME

in YOU and YOU and YOU, with you, for you, through YOU, by YOU, because of YOU, learning you, finding you, loving YOU, helping YOU to find you, and I found me.

HAPPY BIRTHDAY TO SIXTEEN-YEAR-OLD MIKE, WHO DROPPED OUT OF SCHOOL TODAY

I knew you were turned off. Why not? "Nobody gives a damn."
You were just one of hundreds. "They could care less who I am."
The school is full of faces. All are masks. Nobody knows
Or cares what anyone is really feeling. Nothing shows.

Oh, you've got smarts; yet, still more hurts. But cover up; be cool
Play it tough and bluff it through. Stay out alot. Play pool.
Behind *your* mask there is much hurt. But you're not one who shares
Yourself with anybody. "What the hell? Who'd help? Who cares?"

Don't you know there isn't anyone can really hide
From everyone? We've talked a bit. I glimpsed the hurt inside.
"I've run away from home alot. Not any more." And then
You added, "Dad said that he wouldn't look for me again."

I couldn't make you feel my faith in you; I couldn't reach
Behind your mask. Oh Mike, if I can't help the hurt, why teach?
Don't you see? I thought if I could show how *I* believe
In you, that you might change your mind today, and wouldn't leave.

Today's the day you are sixteen. You said, "Don't look for me
At school today – or anymore . . ." . . . . I miss you terribly.
And in this birthday wish I send, the thought that runs all through
Is: You ARE someone special. Please, dear Mike, *believe* in YOU.

Love,
Mrs. J.

SHAKE IT OFF

He yelled, “I’m through!” and walked away,
And said he’d quit the stupid play;
He didn’t like it anyway.
(His friends explained his girl had broken up with him
that very day.)

She frowned and pouted, “Sorry, I
Can’t get the mood; I just can’t try
Today.” She went off for a cry.
(Her mom had “grounded” her for two full weeks. I found
that was why.)

Dear Young, you’ll learn the world won’t stop
Because your fortunes take a drop.
The show goes on; the treadmill spins;
And only he who jumps up, shakes it off, and gets back on it
wins.

THE BEAT

Coiled steel.
A spring.
Trembling.
Burning.
Electric.
Tormented energy
Straining
to
Shatter . . .
Smash

The one who stands,
Taunting, Defying
This coiled spring
of
Anger . . . Fear . . . Shame.
boy-boy-boy.
hurt . . .
huRT . . .
HURT.

I hold him back.
In this sinewy black boy,
under the steel,
I feel the hurt . . . huRT . . .
HURT . . .
The Soul beat
of the Black Man.

The beat . . . beAT . . . BEAT . . .
Pounding the ANGER.
THROBBING the indignity.
boy-boy-boy-
hurt . . .
huRT . . .
HURT.

The beat courses through the steel
Into me.
I *am* the beat.
It is *me*.

To the White Boy,
Standing over
the
Black
Coiled
Steel,
Taunting. Defying,
I cry, in anguish,
"You don't know, do you?
DO YOU?
For God's sake,
Sit down."

ARCHIE

I told Second Period about ARCHIE last week –
(To illustrate a point was why) –
told them how I loved him desperately,
because of the Robert Mitchum dimple in his chin,
the promissory note in his voice,
the devilish light in his eye
that held unspoken, wild promises for *me*.
And how – all along – I think I knew
that I wouldn't have known what to *do*
with ARCHIE,
had I gotten him.

In second period, I told them
how once, in eleventh grade, ARCHIE smudged charcoal
on my cheek
from his magnificent face –
(I couldn't remember how *his* smudge got there
In the first place.) –
How I wrote in my diary that night: "HUBA! HUBA!"
and was delirious for . . . . going-on a week,
'til I saw ARCHIE in the cafeteria on Tuesday, hugging Joan,
who always said what was just right,
and knew how to hold her own
with a guy like ARCHIE,
(which I never did.)

To make my parable clear,
I told Second Period how I languished all year,
dreaming of how it could be
with ARCHIE,
adorable,
devilish,
Continental, Man-About-Town, B.M.O.C.,
and Reach-for-the-Moon, Trip-over-my-Big-Feet-Me,
the LOVE-SICK KID.

I told them how there were some –
(Dick and Teddy . . . and some) –
who would have liked me, had there been a chance.
(They'd have prob'ly been fun.)
But I never knew,
because ARCHIE was *my* face-in-the-sun,
my one-way, never-come-true romance.

That year, the things that I used to do
were: write to my diary of ARCHIE . . . alot;
dream secret dreams of ARCHIE . . . alot;
wish Dick or Teddy were ARCHIE . . . alot.

(I was a stupid kid.)

If you wonder whether Second Period *got* the point . . .
Or not . . . .
I'd say . . . . they did.

THE HOLE-PUNCHERS

I used to have some hole-punchers.
Fancy or costly they were not.
But they *were* nice, because – mostly –
They punched *nice* holes.
Then, too . . . boastly,
It's not just *everyone*,
Who has hole-punchers of her very own.
You know,
I really liked those hole-punchers - alot.

So . . .
There was this girl in class
Who asked for the brief loan
Of my hole-punchers.
She wanted to punch out
    Little
    Round
    Paper
    Pieces
To throw up in the air
At the ball game that night.
That was all right.
I didn't care.
But later that day they were gone,
And I didn't know where.
Then somebody said, "Wait a minute! Hey!
That girl that was punching out
    Little
    Round
    Paper
    Pieces
To throw up in the air
At the ball game. *She* took them away."

So I went to find her.
And I did, and said loudly: "Ahem!

Where are my hole-punchers, please?
Do you have them?"
And just as cool and at ease,
She said, "Oh! I know!
They are in my locker.
I will bring them to you."
I said happily, "Do!
Good! I wish you would!"

But . . . . she didn't.

Next day I saw her again.
I said sternly; "Ahem!
Where are my hole-punchers, please?
Do you still have them?"
And just as cool and at ease,
She said, "Oh! I know!
They are at home.
I will bring them to you."
I said hopefully, "Do.
Good. I wish you would."

But . . . . she didn't.

The next day she came to my room,
And asked me to sign her release
So she could go to this other school.
So I did. Then I said sadly: "I believe
You still have my hole-punchers.
May I have them, please, before you leave?"
And just as cool and at ease,
She said, "I'll be back tomorrow.
I will bring them to you."
I said, desperately, "Do.
Good. I *really* wish you would."

But . . . . she didn't.

She went right on, just as cool,
To that other school the very next day,
Went right on her cool, easy way
To a school that was mostly black; she was white.
And that very same night
On the news – one of those on-the-school-scene interviews –
There SHE was, propounding her views
On LOVE,
And TRUST,
And UNDERSTANDING,
And wonderful things like that
Between black and white and everyone.
She said she wanted to work on getting all those things done,
And she hoped she would and wanted always to be
Remembered as the girl who believed
In LOVE,
And TRUST,
And UNDERSTANDING.

It certainly did *sound* good.
I reckon everyone who saw and heard
Thought, "My word!
What a wonderful, sincere girl!
Just *hear* how she talks
About LOVE,
And TRUST,
AND UNDERSTANDING,
And wonderful things like that!"

But all *I* could think was:
That girl took my hole-punchers,
And left me flat.
For I figured it out, you see;
She never *meant* to bring them back to me.
So that's how *I'LL* remember her.
She will go down in my book
As the girl
Who took
My hole-punchers.

RATED "X"

I'm pretty broad-minded about unorthodox dress,
and long hair and beards and things
that lots of folks think are a mess.
And I think scraggly-looking blue jeans are O.K.,
and shirts that say: DON'T TREAD ON ME

or

EVEN IF I'M WRONG
I'M STILL HUMAN

or

LOVE ME, BABY.

And I like sandals,
and dirty, open-toed tennis shoes are fine.
But I *do* think, maybe, somebody ought to draw the line
at some of the . . . . . SCANDALS
young ladies wear to school,
that are not only NOT . . .
academically oriented. No chance.
What they are . . . I'd say . . . as in pants
Is HOT,
and SEXY.
Take, for instance, those slacks
that are split up the fronts most of the way,
and most of the way up in the backs.
And I have nothing, *personally*, against hot pants
for a picnic, or that kind of a situation.
But when a young lady wears them to school,
and you can see that little roll in back, you know,
why, I think it tends to break her classmates' concentration.
I mean . . . .

Young men *do* have
certain, natural
impulses.
And when a young lady wears shorts to school,
that are almost no shorts at all;
Or wears kind of thin blouses
with nothing underneath . . .
Well . . . it arouses –
(oh, I'm certain the young men – ENJOY) –
but it does make it difficult for a young man to concentrate,
or even *breathe!*
(When *I* see stuff like that, for heaven's sake, I can't *concentrate,*
and *I'm* not even a BOY!)

Honestly, I don't believe a Judge would keep on saying
we infringe on kids' rights
when we tell them what they can't wear –
(drawing the line only at apparel too short, or
see-through, or tight) –
if that Judge would come *one* time and sit in my class –
(he'd have to be over eighteen, or accompanied by a
parent or adult guardian),
well, he'd change his mind about a kid's "right,"
if he'd just sit there in class,
and watch all those sweet, young things
showing
their

lack of discretion.

TO A LOST YOUNG FRIEND

There's hollow laughter in your world. No light.
No feeling left of wonder. No surprise
  To help you grow a glow inside.
  I *need* to know your world. I've tried
To empty all the sunlight from *my* eyes.

I need to go with you into your darkness,
To crawl with you into your dismal cell.
  I MUST. I have to understand
  The way it is in your dark land,
Your never-nothing-nowhere private hell.

I reach for you across your sea of sadness.
You clutch my hand and pull me down with you.
  All drowning, now in cold despair
  I gasp for Hope – it isn't here.
Warm laughter? Love? And God? They're not there, too.

Three days I smother in that lonely prison,
With only wells of emptiness ahead . . .
  Just darkness closing in on me,
  Just numbing, cold futility,
All images of happy things – just dead.

Then – suddenly – somehow – my bonds are loosened.
Released, I soar above the monstrous bier.
  I breathe again; I feel the sun.
  I laugh. I love. I hope. And then
I turn. I scream for you. You cannot hear.

I cannot help you now. I cannot reach you.
But someday, when your lonely course is run,
  Because you know I understand,
  You'll reach for me; you'll clutch my hand,
And let me help you out into the sun.

TURN AROUND'S FAIR PLAY

We watched a film one day.
It was called, "Why Punctuate."
It was a boring show,
A "sleeper" . . . *awf'ly* slow.

We turned the thing around,
And watched it all *backwards* then.
Off the track, a bit,
And . . . suddenly . . . a HIT!

We all laughed – quite alot,
Because it was really fun.
Which, (I say with no hesitation),
Movies on punctuation
Frequently are NOT.
(I can't think of even *one*.)

I wondered what I'd say
Should a School Board member appear,
And angrily demand:
"What IS going ON in here??????"

I would have smiled and said,
(With not even one reservation):
"We are watching a movie today –
Backwards – on punctuation.
We like it better *this* way;
It's a rather refreshing change.
Do pull up a chair and stay."

If he'd have left us then,
Impatiently shaking his head,
Muttering, "Strange. *Very* strange,"
And looking despairingly grim . . . .
. . . .
I'd have felt very *sorry* for him.

MIRROR, MIRROR, ON THE WALL

I crown you with "A."
You look in the mirror
And see the smartest one of all,
You "A" person, you.
You LIKE you!
No wonder you do,
"A" person.

I brand you with "D."
You look in the mirror,
And see you are almost nothing at all,
You "D" person, you.
Maybe you did not try;
Maybe you do not care.
You did? You do?
I see why you do not LIKE you,
Just a bit more than nothing,
"D" person.

I demolish you with "F."
You look in the mirror
And see the dumbest one of all,
You "F" person, you.
Almost always you did not try.
Did you *ever* care?
In the first grade?
The second? The third?
Did you care when you could not read?
Or understand?
When you learned to never raise your hand
And they passed you by?
Is that when you stopped *trying* to try,
Because you knew you were a Failure,
"F" person?

UNTIL TOMORROW

Ah, how you love,
    you two –
    one silhouette
    against the lockers there.
What secret world you share,
What dreams beget –
    in her eyes,
    in his smile.
How you love, you two,
    faces almost touching,
    eyes touching.
Ah, how you find
    warmth,
    shelter,
In the quiet ring
of your love.
What safeness, now, you bring
    to her,
    to him.
It's such a big world, isn't it?
    It's cold outside,
    and not so kind.
        Never mind.
Wrap yourself in his smile.
Snuggle in the warm of her eyes.
And love forever, you two.
    or, anyway,
        until tomorrow,
          or the next day.

STAND BY

On the back of my classroom door,
written in a big, black
magic marker scrawl:

I GET THE FEELING
EVERYONE SEEMS to HATE ME

There's more.
Under that:

HATE vs LOVE
HATE WINS by A MILE

That's not all.
In the same scrawl
in tiny little letters:

Jimmy loves Debby

Jimmy is short,
and fat,
and kind of ugly.

Sometimes, he acts "smart."
Sometimes . . . he tries to smile.

He loves pretty, little Debby,
and everyday, Pretty Debby breaks his heart.

Debby doesn't love Jimmy.
Debby doesn't *like* Jimmy.

So Jimmy's miserable, and nothing comes out right.

He says DUMB things when she's there.
He does DUMB things when she's there.

And, because he is fat and miserable and kind of ugly,
they seem dumber, I guess, than they might.

Oh, I *WISH* I could make Debby care!
I WISH I could make her

SMILE
at Jimmy,
LOVE
Jimmy.

I smile at Jimmy.
I love Jimmy.
But I'm not Debby.

******

So I must stand by
and watch Jimmy

HATING
himself

For saying DUMB things,
and doing DUMB things;

For being short,

and fat,

and kind of ugly,

and I can't help Jimmy out . . .
I mustn't try,
for Jimmy is on his own.

It *hurts* – growing up.
It *hurts* – standing by.

But that's what growing up,
and that's what *being* grown

are
about.

TABOO

Sometimes – not often – something comes along,
A miracle of sorts that looms so bright
There are no words to tell it with, because
The words would only make it come out wrong,
No matter how you try to shape them right,
And make them say the way it really was . . .
How sensitive . . . how delicate . . . how warm.

But still, you *have* to tell it; have to try
To write it, cage experience in form
So someone else can share this thing with you;
Can feel it, live it with you, and can know
The very special way it was . . . and why.

One morning, rather early in the day,
I worked collecting school books in my room
To send for final counting at year's end.
I was alone. Alone, except for one,
(He didn't have to be in class just then),
So he was there with me. A thin boy, tall,
Just quiet, for just quiet was his way.
A very gentle one – my young, black friend –
Who wrote things like this down in class for me:
"We have to love each other and be kind,
And care. All men are brothers. All."
And this he lived; you'd pass him in the hall
And feel that very gentleness in him.
(You have to know, and feel, all this, you see
Before you'll ever understand what came.)
So there we were, my quiet friend and I,
With me – all clutched, uptight, out of my mind.
(My books were due, *past* due, in fact. And now
I fought the losing fight to beat back time.)
I stacked more piles on piles; he stood behind –
A presence . . . easy . . . comforting somehow,
A contrast to my frenzy was his calm.

To rearrange a pile just then, I knelt.
(He couldn't, though he offered, help me. So
He just stood close by watching me). And then
To interrupt my race with time, I felt
His hand upon my shoulder, firm, yet light.

I *know* what thoughts now push and rush on you . . .

TABOO

A black boy touch a white?

SHOCK!

My shame is that, at first, I felt that, too.
What would come next? What should I do?
A black boy touch a white? A woman? Me?

. . . .

Please God, help them to see
How light his touch, how gently firm, how *right* . . .
God, *make* them see
How suddenly, then, suddenly I knew
We were not black or white, or woman-man;
Here, we were brothers. This was all that's true;
All meaning; where all love, respect began.

And when I stood again, his hand was gone.
Had I been dreaming? Was it really there?
I asked my friend to take some books somewhere.
I trembled, then, when I was all alone.
I thought again of all that is "taboo";
I thought again of all that's real and true.
And then, I *knew* a miracle had been,
A tiny, little miracle right there.

I wanted just to weep, or laugh; To share
The beauty with someone; to shout out loud

The wonder of this thing. I didn't dare.
For nobody, I knew, would understand
    But God.
And why tell Him? For He was there.

A LITTLE THING

I saw something today.
It was at school; I saw it in "B" wing.
It was a world . . . a universe . . . forever . . .
But just a little thing
You probably would hardly ever see
Or notice – nine days out of ten.

Two boys talking in a narrow hall . . .
Each turned away to go;
And then
A smile . . .
Just warm, just friends was all.
They touched hands,
As boys do – boys who are friends.
"So long, pal.
See ya' in a while."
The black hand glanced the white
There in the dusty hall.
And that was all.
You see? It was a quiet, little thing –
I told you so.

The one that passed me then,
(The one with the white hand),
Looked up at me – an easy, open look,
And in his eyes – a little, warming smile
That said . . . "Oh, don't you know?
We'll be all right."

A PARABLE

It seemed to be like any other day.
We sat and ate our lunch in the small room,
We teachers. This – our chance to chat awhile;
The conversation shifting this – that way,
From ups-and-downs at school to those at home;
No portent there; no warning that would come
To make you sick, to decimate a smile.
The problem: field mice coming from the cold
For food and warmth into a teacher's house.
Another teacher spoke. The tale she told
Was this: She and another teacher heard
A clatter in their bathroom; rushed in, found
A small squirrel splashing in the toilet bowl.
"And so," she calmly said, "we flushed him down."

We others listened; no one said a word.

"But up he bobbed," she said. "He spluttered, splashed.
I ran and got a shovel; held him down.
You should have seen him duck and bob about,
But I held fast," she boasted, proudly grim.
"And finally, I held him down until
His struggling stopped. And then, we threw him out.
My, we were glad to rid ourselves of him!"

We, who listened, sat there, numb and still.

I felt so sick, so horrified, so weak,
I tried to but, at first, I could not speak.
The others who were there were silent, too.
I sighed at last, "I'd kind of hoped that you
Were going to tell us what you'd planned to do
Was use that shovel just to help him free."
Another teacher softly said, "That's cruel."
I didn't look at them, nor they at me.
I left then; for I would not, could not stay.

I have not been the same, not since that day
Listening in the teachers' room at school.
I can not shake the heavy memory
Of those two teachers and their "victory."
That teacher and her friend – the same ones who
Broke that small squirrel so relentlessly,
Held him 'till his struggling was all through –
They teach our young . . . . ones – sometimes – who rebel
And seem all out of place and struggle, too,
Drowning in a world they can't condone.

I wonder, now, what do those teachers do
With struggling, strangling youngsters who must flail
Against some values they can't see as true?
Do they just push them down relentlessly,
Hold them there, until their struggling's done,
And they lie still, their fight, their spirit gone,
Exterminated by the shovel of
  That unrelenting, grim authority?

HANDLE WITH CARE

Yesterday
you brought to me
the tender green shoot
of your young soul,
cradled in a lavender folder,
a yellow daisy picture on the front.
You did not say:
This is Me,
My Soul,
Everything I am . . .
and want to be . . .
and am afraid of . . . and . . . .
You only said,
as you placed it in my hand,
"Would you proofread my poems, please Mrs. J.?"

I took the folder from you, tenderly,
watching your eyes widen as I leafed through
the pages of your Soul.
Understand? was the soft plea in your eyes,
the little tightness around your mouth.
Be gentle. *Please*. Be gentle with my dreams,
the way I love; the way I hurt . . . and hate;
the way I try to put it down onto
the square inch space of blank white paper.
Be gentle. Please. Be gentle.

******

Ah yes, there are mistakes.
The wording, in places, weak;
the ideas . . . nothing new . . . unique.
a misspelled word or two;
cliches . . . a few.

But still . . . .
What I hold here is the tender shoot
of your young climbing soul.

Be gentle?

Yes. Oh, yes. I will.

SO – WHAT HAPPENED TO *YOU*?

We were watching a movie in class,
"The Doll's House," by Henrik Ibsen;
(It was one I hadn't seen.)
All of a sudden – – – – – there was *Frannie Sternhagen*,
Right up there on the screen!
I shouted, "Look! There!
It's Frannie Sternhagen!"
"WHAT?" they cried. "Where?
WHO?"
Who is Frannie Stern . . . WHO?"
"She's Nora, the lead. Up *there*!
On the screen. She's a girl I knew
I'll tell you when the movie's through."

Well, after Nora slammed that famous door,
And it said, "The End,"
And the lights were on once more,
I said, proudly,
"Frannie Sternhagen was my friend.
We went to the second, third, and fourth grades
At the same school –
Me and Frannie Sternhagen.
I used to go to her house,
For her birthday party, as a rule,
And eat creamed chicken and peas and rice,
And ice cream and cake. What's more – "

(I hated to be a Name Dropper, BUT) –
"Sometimes, Frannie Sternhagen –
(More than just once or twice) –
"Invited *me* and Ally Bean, who lived next door,
Over for lunch. And wow,
Look at Frannie Sternhagen NOW!
'Making educational films;
And that's just the beginning.
She's been in a bunch of New York plays,"
(I read that in the Alumni Review),
"And – by the way –
She won a Tony Award, too.
Besides *that*, she's been on T.V.
'Looks like there's absolutely *no* stopping
My friend, the celebrity,
Frannie Sternhagen."

There was this l o n g p a u s e.

Finally, somebody said to me,
"So – – – – what happened to *YOU*?"
(And that's what *I* get for name-dropping!)

What happened to *me*?
Well, for what I do, I *don't* get applause.
I won't get my name up in lights. That's true.
And my students don't think much of what happened to me –
(Being a school teacher *is* sort of low-key.)
But . . . honestly . . .
I think what happened to me is pretty all right, too.
I really do.